SOLITUDE

POEMS AND QUOTES

SHREERAJ MENON

Contents

Contents

Contents

Contents

Contents

Preface

This book consists of some of the poems and Quotes written by the author on the theme of Love, Nature and general day to day aspects of life. There are some inspirational quotes too. Love includes Love found, Love lost and love re-awakened. Similarly, Nature consists of the importance of nature and how people mis-utilize the nature to their own advantages without going for the aftereffects. General consists of the general aspects of life which goes on with people and the surroundings.

Acknowledgements

I would like to thank my friends who inspired me in writing the Poems and Quotes which I used to say out and forget it. I would also like to thank Your Quote platforms and all its members and groups for allowing me and inspiring me to write my contents on its platform. I would also like to thank Notion Press and all its members who allowed me to publish my contents through their platform and the time-to-time guidance which they gave me to correct my errors.

1. Allow your heart

Allow your heart

Allow your heart to blossom
Like a flower become awesome

Let it flourish and love bloom
Never back down and gloom

— Raj

2. In the autumn of life

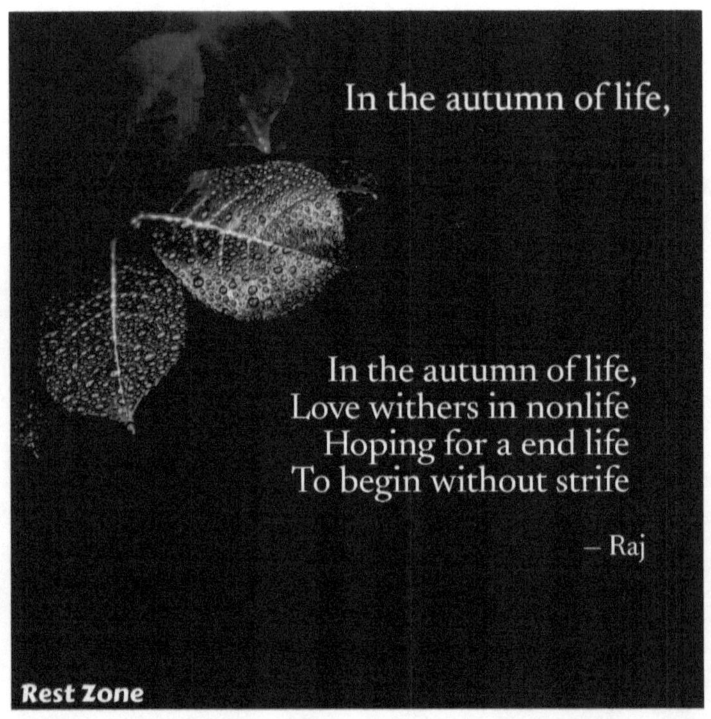

In the autumn of life,

In the autumn of life,
Love withers in nonlife
Hoping for a end life
To begin without strife

— Raj

Rest Zone

3. What's beautiful about love

What's beautiful about love

Beauty of love can't be defined
It should be felt and confined
Love can't be expressed in words
It's divine and not something absurd
Love has a deep meaning inside
People who knows never search outside

— Raj

4. Behind some doors

• 4 •

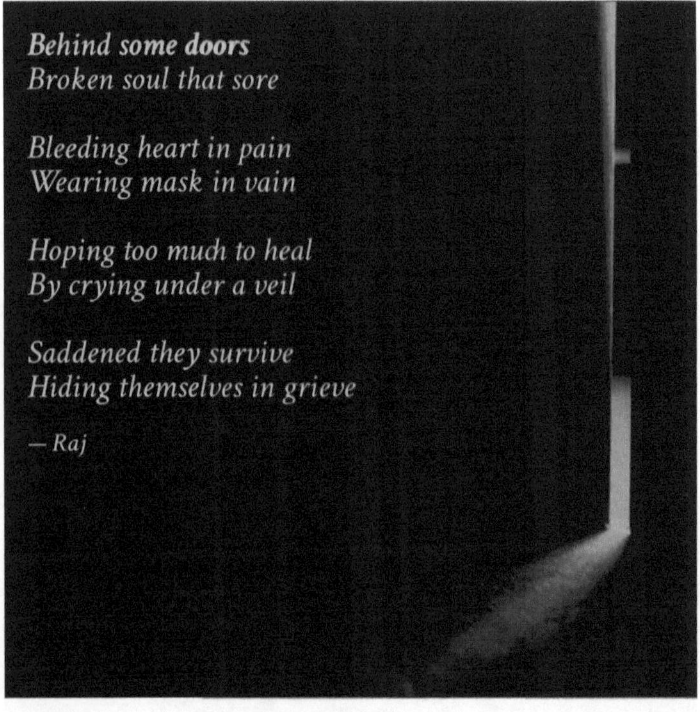

Behind some doors
Broken soul that sore

Bleeding heart in pain
Wearing mask in vain

Hoping too much to heal
By crying under a veil

Saddened they survive
Hiding themselves in grieve

— Raj

5. Some relationships are

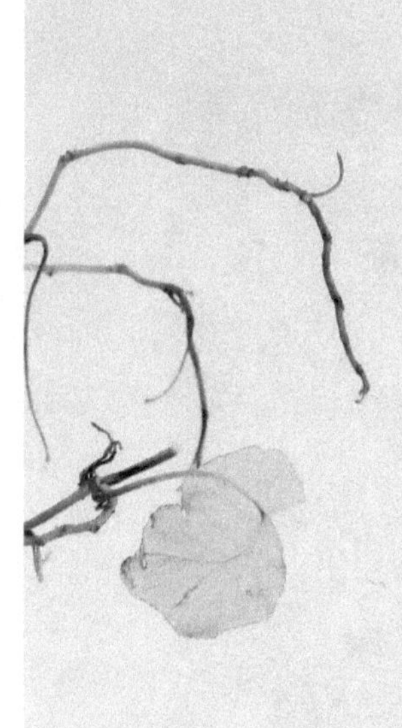

Some relationships are
like those dead flowers

Which blooms for a while
And shed's forever

They are just passer bys
Who comes and goes forever

— Raj

6. A book knows

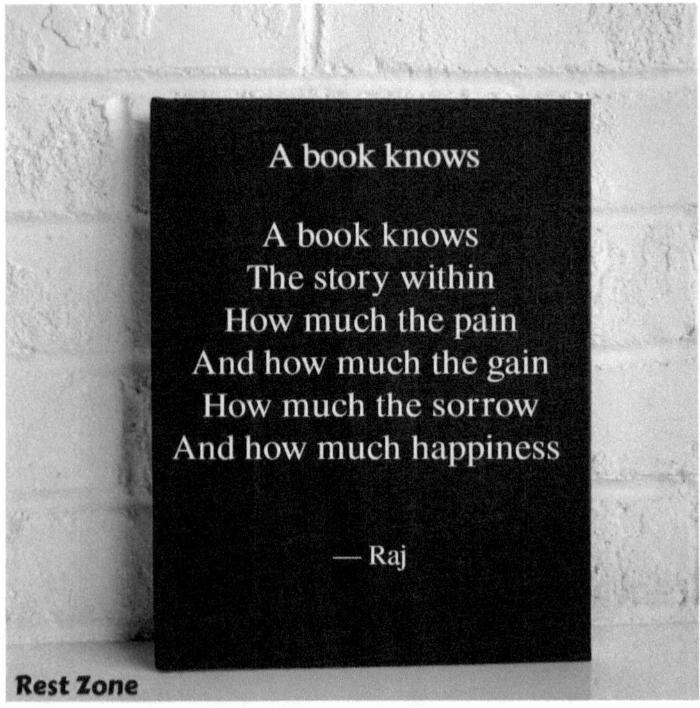

A book knows

A book knows
The story within
How much the pain
And how much the gain
How much the sorrow
And how much happiness

— Raj

Rest Zone

7. On the canvas of my life

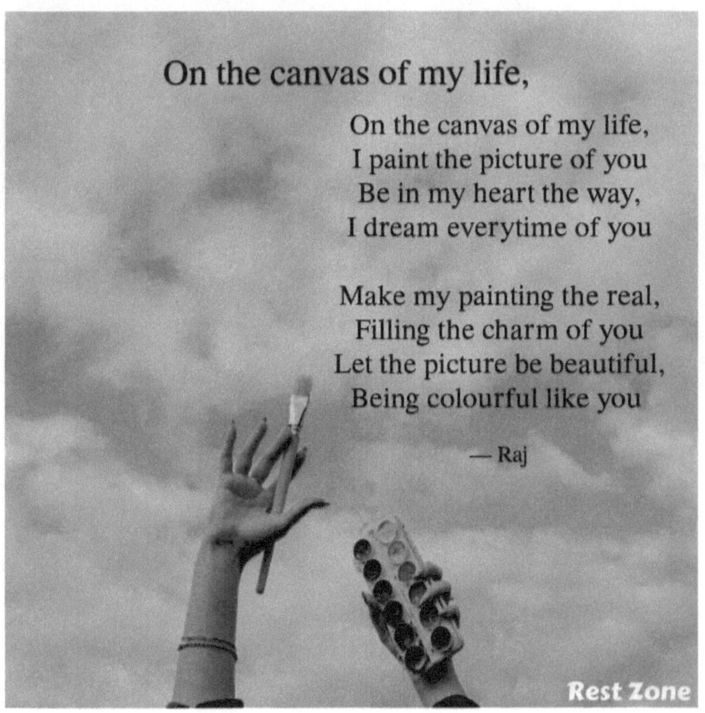

On the canvas of my life,
On the canvas of my life,
I paint the picture of you
Be in my heart the way,
I dream everytime of you

Make my painting the real,
Filling the charm of you
Let the picture be beautiful,
Being colourful like you

— Raj
Rest Zone

8. Asking who are you?

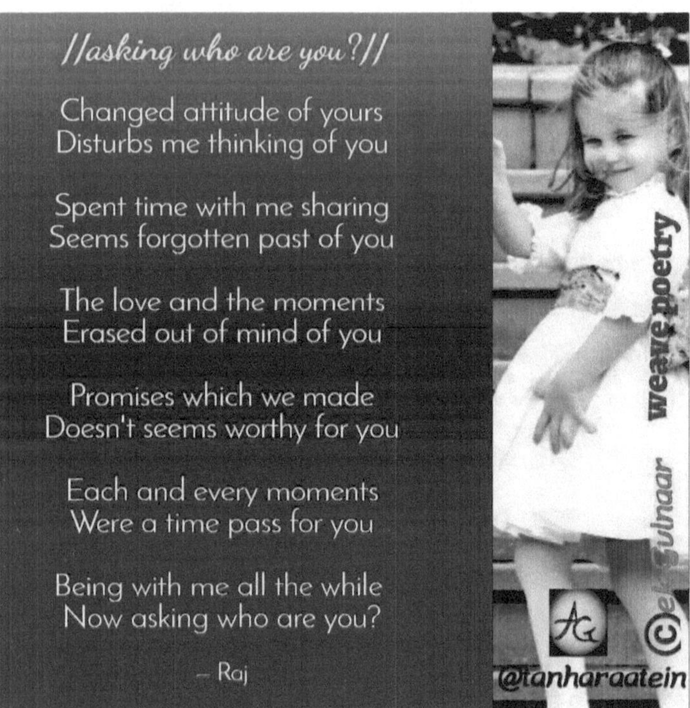

//asking who are you?//

Changed attitude of yours
Disturbs me thinking of you

Spent time with me sharing
Seems forgotten past of you

The love and the moments
Erased out of mind of you

Promises which we made
Doesn't seems worthy for you

Each and every moments
Were a time pass for you

Being with me all the while
Now asking who are you?

– Raj

weave poetry
©el Gulnaar
@tanharaatein

9. The darker the night

The darker the night
The clearer the sight

The stronger the might
The fiercer the fight

The denser the love
The deeper the crave

The quicker the start
The weaker the heart

— Raj

10. Dear Painful Memories

Dear Painful Memories,
Erase and free my worries
It doesn't works any good
Always spoils every mood
Let me to let go and move
Future lies ahead all above

– Raj

11. When You're afraid

When you're afraid
of disappointment
don't ever back off
By awakening a ray
of hope in the heart
Let's move forward

— Raj

Rest Zone

12. Don't Follow

Don't follow
Don't follow
The footsteps of others
Make your own
Footsteps that feathers

Let people follow
The imprints of yours
Make your own
Glory that people follows

— Raj

13. Engrossed

मग्न / Engrossed

Engrossed in your dream
I feel like having an ice cream

Pacing the beat of my heart
Begin loving you from the start

Keeping all the strings open
I invite you to my life often

— Raj

Rest Zone

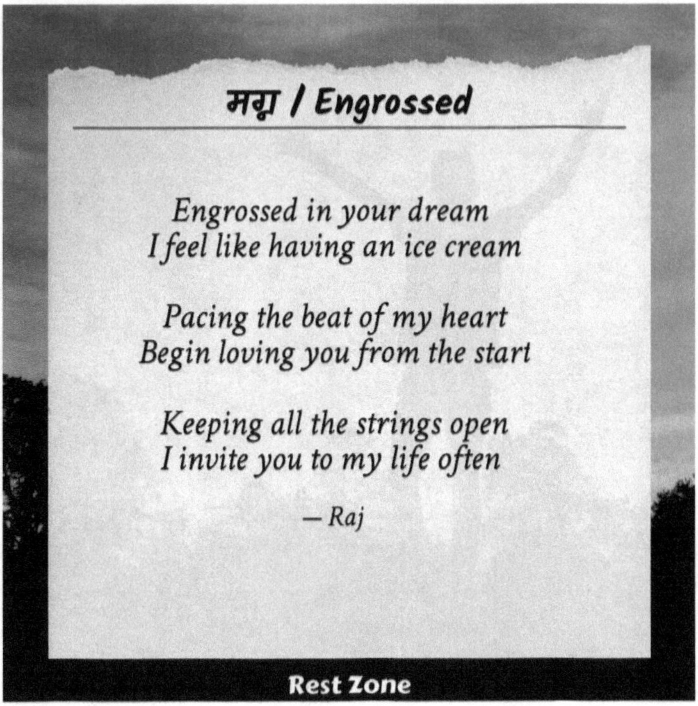

14. Even if the world ends

Rest Zone
Even if the world ends,
Love for you will never fade
Even if It gives wounds,
Love will protect you in shade

— Raj

15. To excel in life

To excel in life,

To excel in life one should have
courage and destiny
How ever you fly high in the sky
landing is definite

— Raj

16. Experience gives you

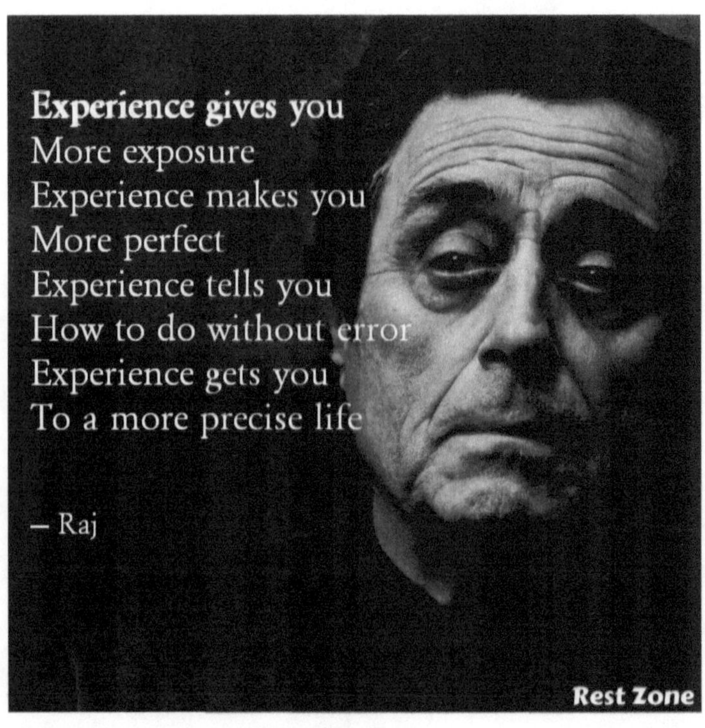

Experience gives you
More exposure
Experience makes you
More perfect
Experience tells you
How to do without error
Experience gets you
To a more precise life

— Raj

Rest Zone

17. Lucky are the ones

Lucky are the ones who
Fell in true love and got it
Lucky are the ones who
Got untrue love and lost it

Unadulterated love can be
Found only in unmatured kids
Love the kids to the most
And feel the love in return for it

— Raj

18. Fragrance

#NaPoWriMo15
~ Fragrance ~

The fragrance of love
Is found very rare
The chao's of the world
And hatred everywhere

The heart is yearning
For the magic to begin
To end the war game
and where humanity reign

— Raj

Rest Zone

19. The fragrance of your love

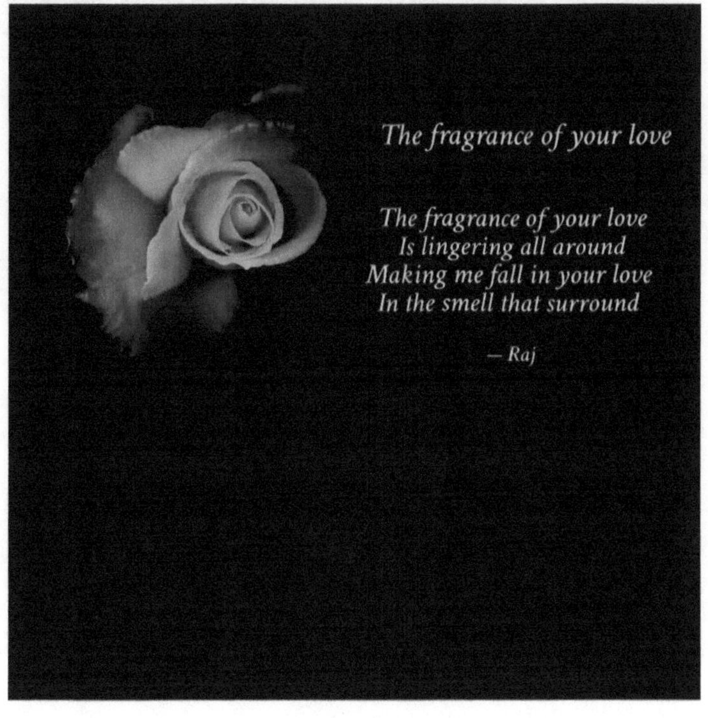

The fragrance of your love

The fragrance of your love
Is lingering all around
Making me fall in your love
In the smell that surround

— Raj

20. Friendships break when

Friendships break when

Friendships break when
There is a breach of trust
With all misunderstandings
That remains without solutions

– Raj

Rest Zone

21. Heart aches when

Heart aches when our beloved goes away
Whether expressed or not the pain resides

— Raj

22. Not all desires

• 22 •

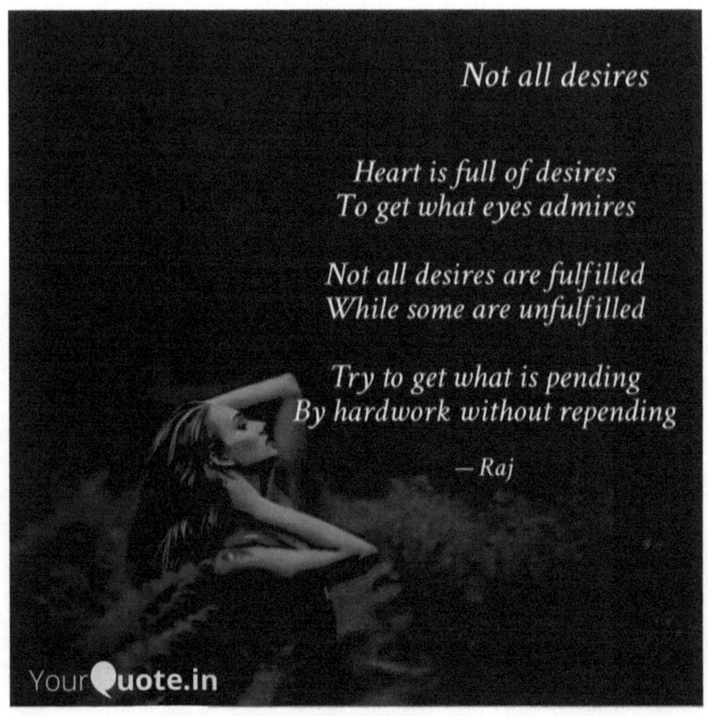

Not all desires

Heart is full of desires
To get what eyes admires

Not all desires are fulfilled
While some are unfulfilled

Try to get what is pending
By hardwork without repending

— Raj

YourQuote.in

23. The heart can't stop

The heart can't stop
The heart can't stop
Beating non-stop
Making love with you
Energy flowing atop

Whether you like or not
It will keep beating a lot
Spreading consciousness
Of the Love on the spot

— Raj

24. A good life is not

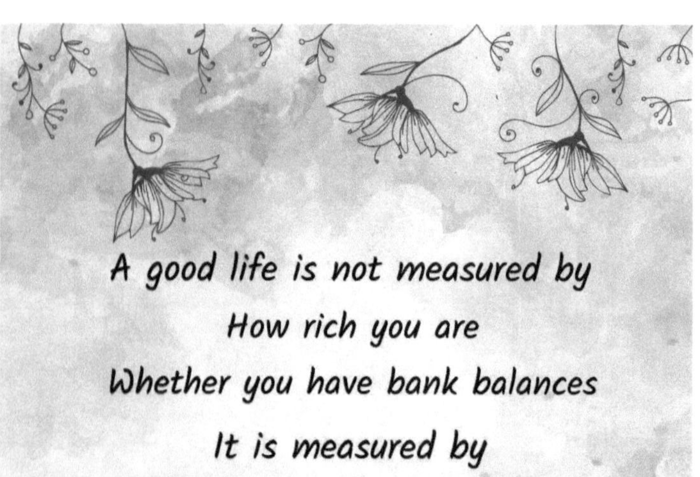

A good life is not measured by
How rich you are
Whether you have bank balances

It is measured by
The way you live peacefully
The ways how people respects your action

— Raj

25. Ignore the ones

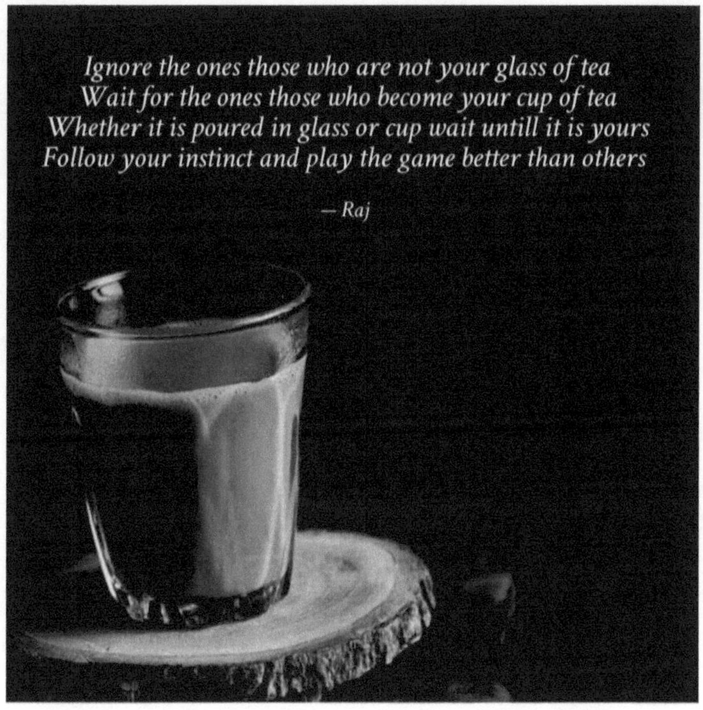

Ignore the ones those who are not your glass of tea
Wait for the ones those who become your cup of tea
Whether it is poured in glass or cup wait untill it is yours
Follow your instinct and play the game better than others

— Raj

26. If I hadn't met you

If I hadn't met you,

If I hadn't met you,
Would have lead a better life

If I hadn't accepted you,
Would have had a better wife

If I wasn't destined you
Wouldn't had lived in a strife

If I wasn't obsessed by you
Wouldn't had so-called antilife

— Raj

27. Yet to explore

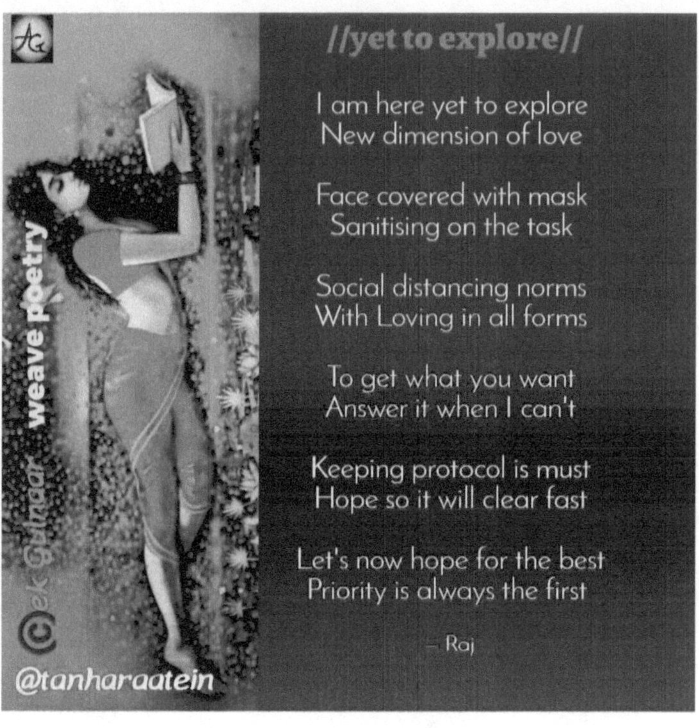
weave poetry
ek gulaar
@tanharaatein
//yet to explore//

I am here yet to explore
New dimension of love

Face covered with mask
Sanitising on the task

Social distancing norms
With Loving in all forms

To get what you want
Answer it when I can't

Keeping protocol is must
Hope so it will clear fast

Let's now hope for the best
Priority is always the first

– Raj

28. I'm not yours

I'm not yours

I know well that I'm not yours
It took a lot of time and years

No matter if I spend all my fears
To think of you without any tears

No matter if I am alone every night
Walking lonely in the moon light

Speaking to the stars in twilight
Spend every moment weighing light

— Raj

29. I like those people

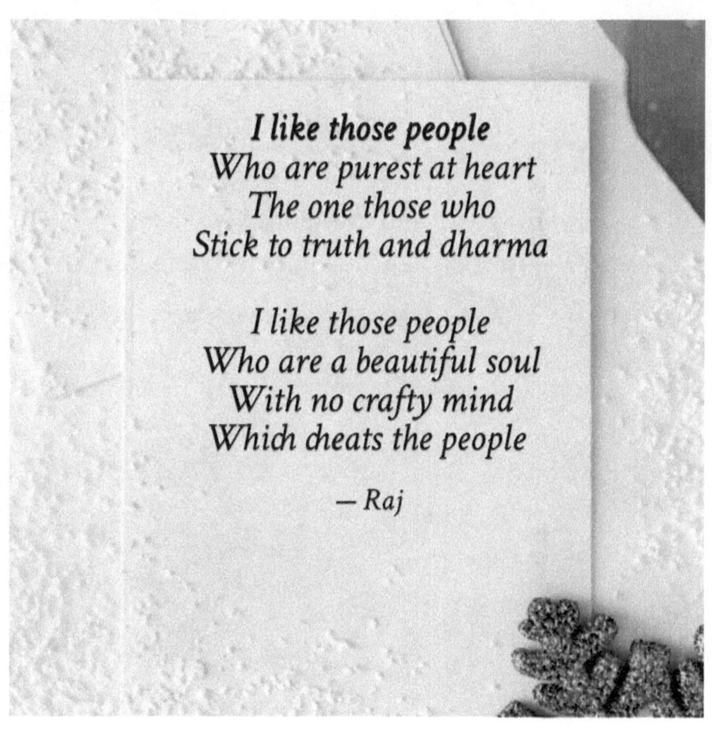

I like those people
Who are purest at heart
The one those who
Stick to truth and dharma

I like those people
Who are a beautiful soul
With no crafty mind
Which cheats the people

— Raj

30. I'm lonely and sad

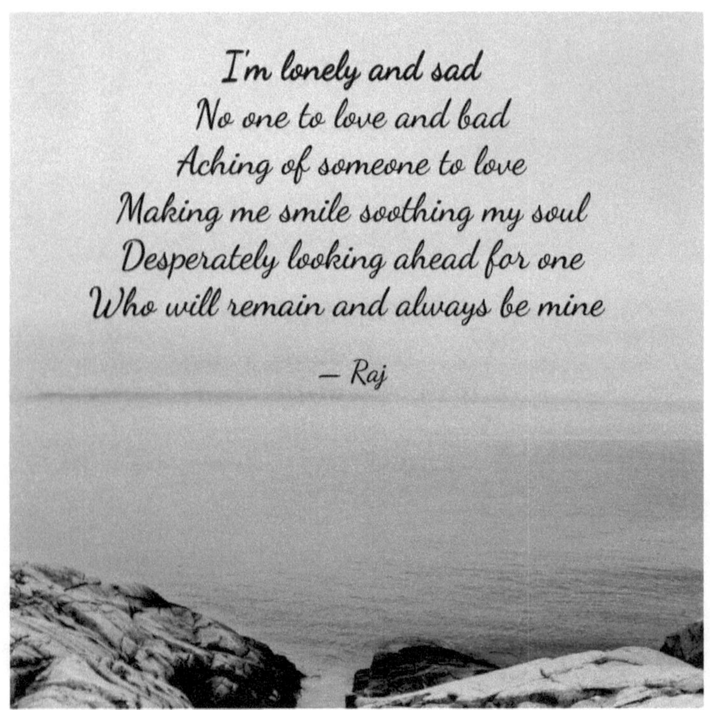

I'm lonely and sad
No one to love and bad
Aching of someone to love
Making me smile soothing my soul
Desperately looking ahead for one
Who will remain and always be mine

— Raj

31. Importance of Happiness

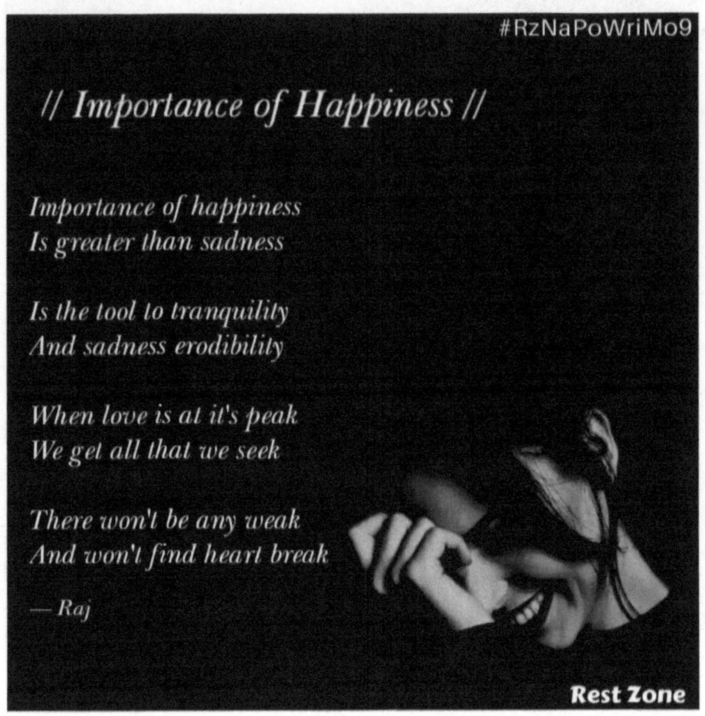

#RzNaPoWriMo9

// Importance of Happiness //

Importance of happiness
Is greater than sadness

Is the tool to tranquility
And sadness erodibility

When love is at it's peak
We get all that we seek

There won't be any weak
And won't find heart break

— Raj

Rest Zone

32. I still have a long way

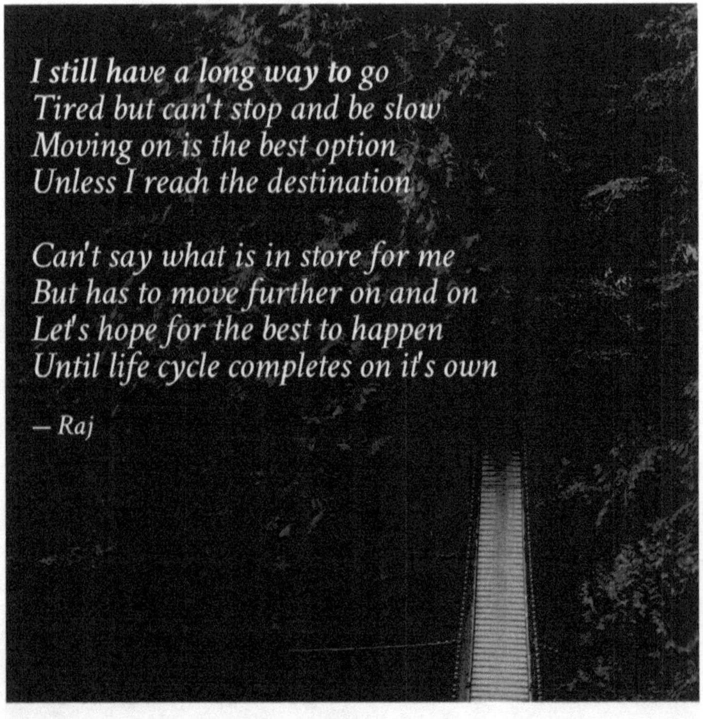

I still have a long way to go
Tired but can't stop and be slow
Moving on is the best option
Unless I reach the destination

Can't say what is in store for me
But has to move further on and on
Let's hope for the best to happen
Until life cycle completes on it's own

— Raj

33. It hurts when someone

It hurts when someone
Leaves you all of a sudden
With all the misunderstandings
Because all they can see is that
it's your fault

It feels good when relationships
That are known to be strained end
Which may leave some hurt
in the heart
But also some hope for a better
tomorrow

— Raj

34. Just one misleading

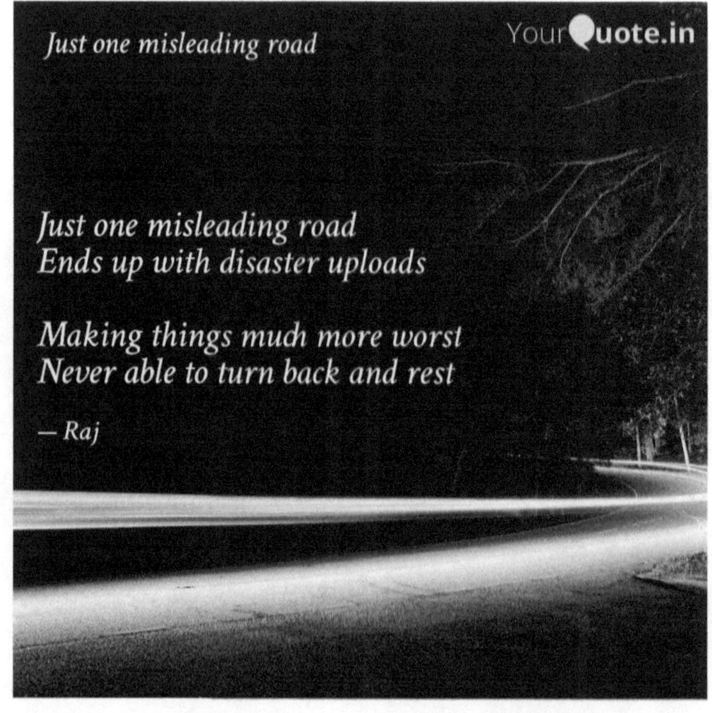

Just one misleading road

YourQuote.in

Just one misleading road
Ends up with disaster uploads

Making things much more worst
Never able to turn back and rest

— Raj

35. Life is hard, but

Life is hard, but

Life is hard, but you have to keep going
The path is difficult, but the destination
has to be achieved

One should have courage to overcome
every difficulty
The path filled with the thorns is to be
overcome by laying flowers

— Raj

36. Life isn't bad

Life isn't bad

Life isn't bad, there is no need to be sad
It goes on in a flow where there is no end
Climb the ladder when ever it is available
Don't hesitate, go ahead until it is stable

— Raj

37. Life is more beautiful

Life is more beautiful when

Life is more beautiful when
There is no fear of death

Live life to the fullest and
Fulfill the never ending desire

— Raj

38. Life is a river

Life is a river

Life is a river
Just flow along
If you feel shiver
Just play along

— Raj

39. Like a caged bird

Like a caged bird,

Like a caged bird
I ache for freedom
Wish to fly high in the sky
Which I get seldom

Here my heart is bond
Where ties comes from
Need to break those ties
And create my kingdom

— Raj

40. Your memories hurt me

• 40 •

Your memories hurt me

Living in the memories
Gives me the aches vast

Your memories hurt me
Making it miserable fast

Forgetting is my hearts desire
Can't make it possibly rest

Always makes havoc in mind
Breaking my heart sect by sect

— Raj

41. Loneliness kills

• 41 •

Loneliness kills

Lonliness kills the chao's inviting peace
Developing the brain in a beautiful way
By improving the energy center's of the
body and creating a peacefull mind

- Raj

42. Love is a boat

• 42 •

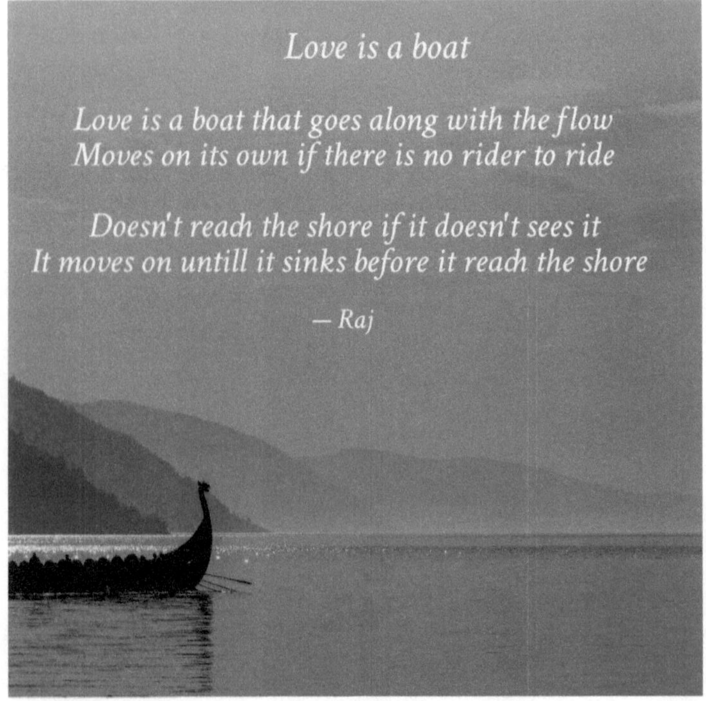

Love is a boat

Love is a boat that goes along with the flow
Moves on its own if there is no rider to ride

Doesn't reach the shore if it doesn't sees it
It moves on untill it sinks before it reach the shore

— Raj

43. Love is that bud

Love is that bud

Love is that bud
Which blooms and shed's

The cycle goes on
Until someone really bed's

Broken heart and deeper pain
Is the side effects which never fades

— Raj

44. Love is like fire

Love is like fire

Love is like fire
It spreads everywhere
Burning everything to ashes
If not handled with care

Love is like sweet
Makes everyone blind
Like more sugar makes diabetic
If not handled with care

Love is a sweet poison
Sweet in the begining and sour later
It not only hurts but kills
If not handled with care

— Raj

45. Love matters more

• 45 •

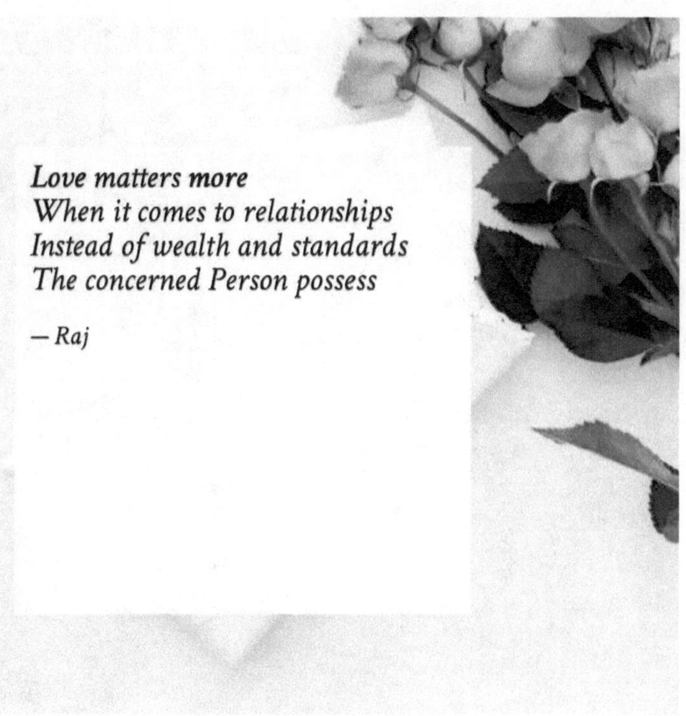

Love matters more
When it comes to relationships
Instead of wealth and standards
The concerned Person possess

— Raj

46. Love is music

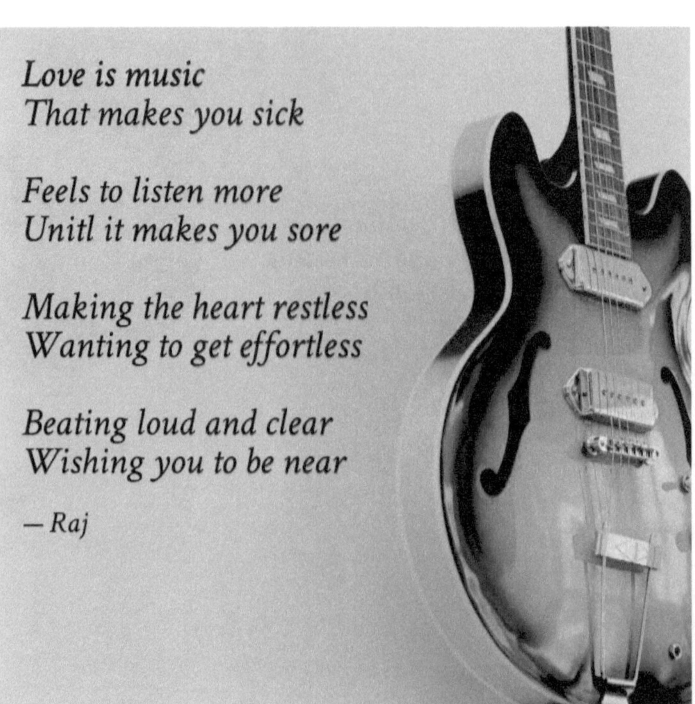
Love is music
That makes you sick

Feels to listen more
Unitl it makes you sore

Making the heart restless
Wanting to get effortless

Beating loud and clear
Wishing you to be near

— Raj

47. Love seems to be a mistake

Love seems to be a mistake

Love seems to be a mistake
Wrongly planted in the heart
It is like a slow sweet poison
That gives only pain in a cart

Being neutral keeps you alive
There is neither love nor hatered
Kill the emotions which you have
And live your life happily ahead

— Raj

48. Meditation and peace are

Meditation and peace are

Meditation and peace are
The back bone of life's existence
Without which it is unable to
Get the desired harmony of cosmic energy

— Raj

49. The moon silently watches

The moon silently watches

The moon silently watches
The star's silently twinkles
The night silently speaks
The never told story remains

The story of the nights dark
Which gives dangerous spark
With all the illegal activities
In the shadow of dark takes part

— Raj

50. The moon in the sky

The moon in the sky

The moon in the sky
Is bright and very coy
Amidst the stars that pry
Twinkling with a sly

Spreading it's own light
Showing the way of life
Sometimes hidden tight
Sometimes cresent sight

— Raj

51. The more lonely you feel

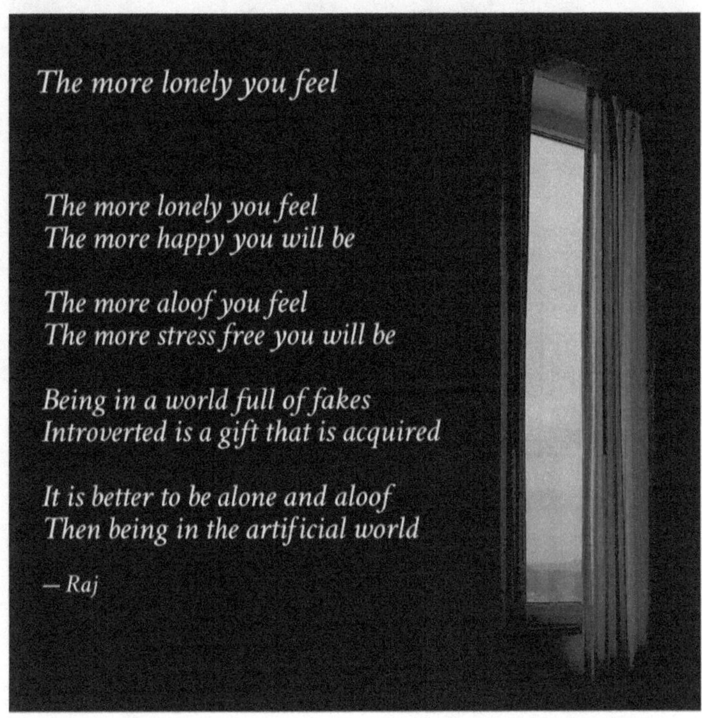

The more lonely you feel

The more lonely you feel
The more happy you will be

The more aloof you feel
The more stress free you will be

Being in a world full of fakes
Introverted is a gift that is acquired

It is better to be alone and aloof
Then being in the artificial world

— Raj

52. Morning comes

Morning comes

Morning comes with new hopes and desires
Afternoon goes off with all the works and welfare's
Evening comes with all tiredness and affairs
Night comes again with deep dreams that fair's
Days and days pass on like this with all time fire's

— Raj

ProverbsW rld

53. My dear beautiful flower

My dear beautiful flower
Wanna see you shower
Sprinkling the holy water
Bloom and never wither

Wanna see smile forever
Sadness should be never
Live life happily as ever
Never be afraid and shiver

— Raj

54. I'm yet to find the one

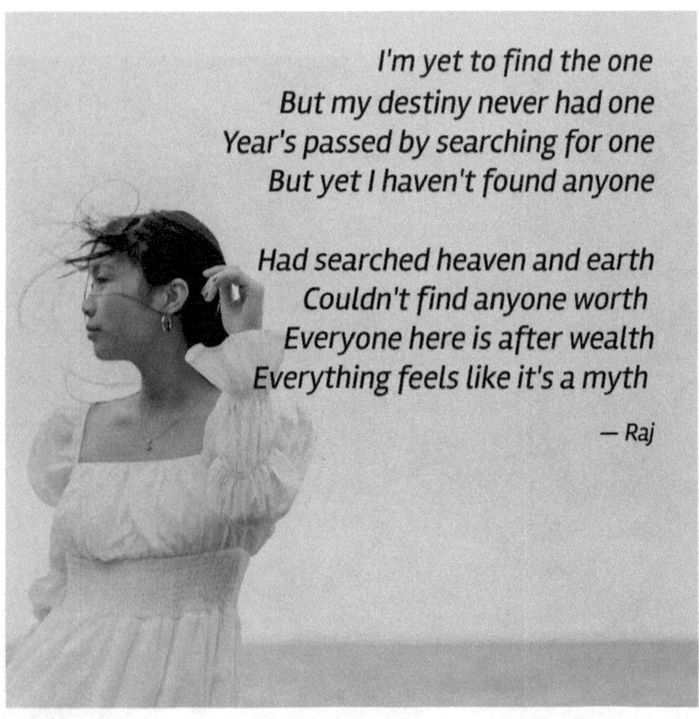
I'm yet to find the one
But my destiny never had one
Year's passed by searching for one
But yet I haven't found anyone

Had searched heaven and earth
Couldn't find anyone worth
Everyone here is after wealth
Everything feels like it's a myth

— Raj

55. Kindness

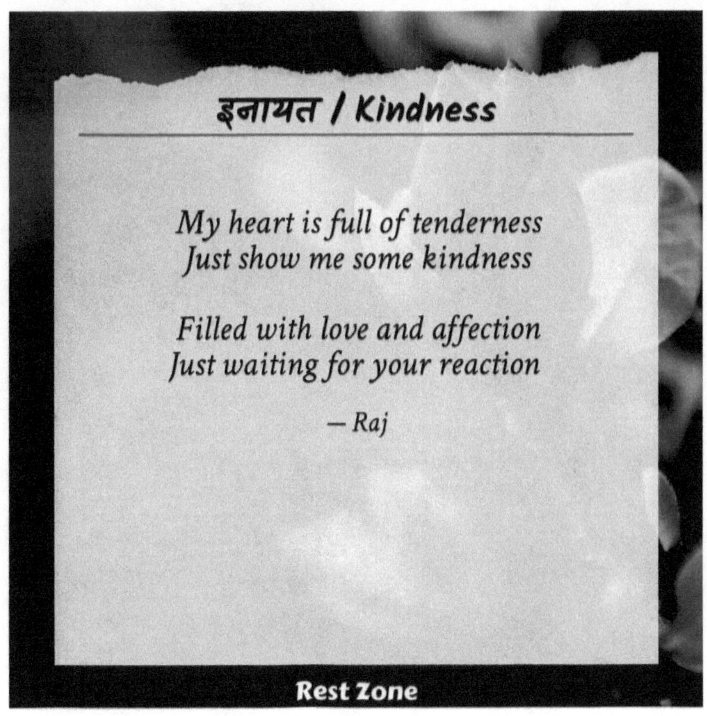

इनायत / Kindness

My heart is full of tenderness
Just show me some kindness

Filled with love and affection
Just waiting for your reaction

— Raj

Rest Zone

56. My heart melts

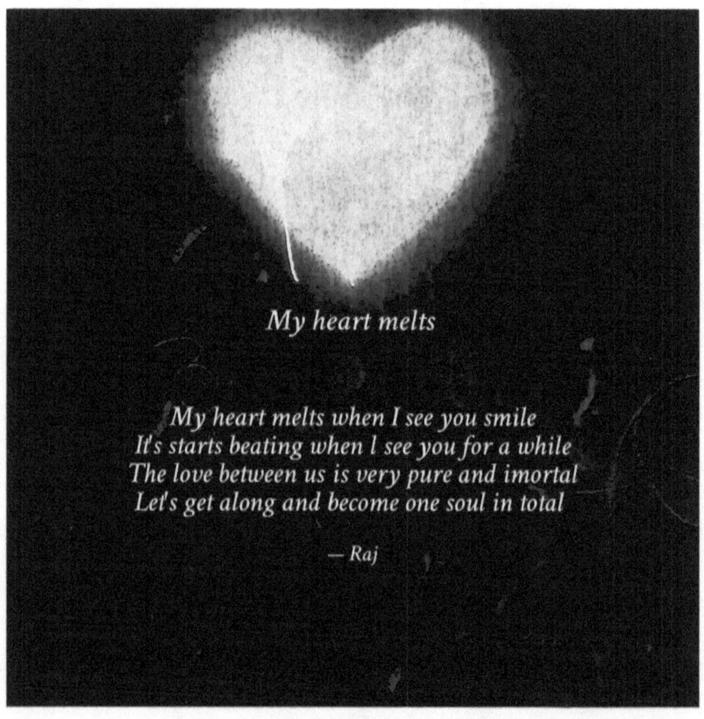
My heart melts

My heart melts when I see you smile
It's starts beating when I see you for a while
The love between us is very pure and imortal
Let's get along and become one soul in total

— Raj

57. My heart sings

My heart sings

My heart sings the song of life
Without fun how much the strife

Longing for love with a smile
Serendipity plays the role wide

— Raj

58. My love wasn't temporary

My love wasn't temporary

My love wasn't temporary
Then why are you in hurry

Let the time tell the story
Then why are you in worry

My love for you is like berry
Let's enjoy it and be merry

In my heart you are the fairy
Would say never get angry

Come let's go and get marry
Before the things get scary

— Raj

59. Peace in my heart

//peace in my heart//

Nature is beautiful
With lot of colours

Saw some butterflies
On a lot of flowers

The scene which I see
Leaves peace in my heart

That is the so called love
Which begins to start

The mist on the mountain
And the greenery everywhere

Feels good to look at the scene
Heart full of love somewhere

– Raj

weavepoetry
©ek Gulzar
tanharaatein

60. You and your love

You and your love
both taught me
Never to trust love
between you and me

Unless you feel love
sensing the divinity
People tends to hide
feelings with serenity

— Raj

61. The night is prettier

The night is prettier when

The night is prettier when you are with me
Moonlight glittering and stars twinkling at me
Blooming love and the climate is favourable
We both together and filled with love and pleasure

— Raj

Rest Zone

62. Nights hurt

Nights hurt

Nights hurts never
Love the darkness

With moon light ever
Sky and the stillness

The flow of cold air
Making the chillness

Cool is the atmosphere
Where there is likeness

— Raj

63. Nobody cares about

Nobody cares about
Nobody cares about
The desires of heart

What ever you think
People always stink

Let go of those ones
Live your life at once

Don't care about others
Just think of only yours

— Raj

64. No matter what happens

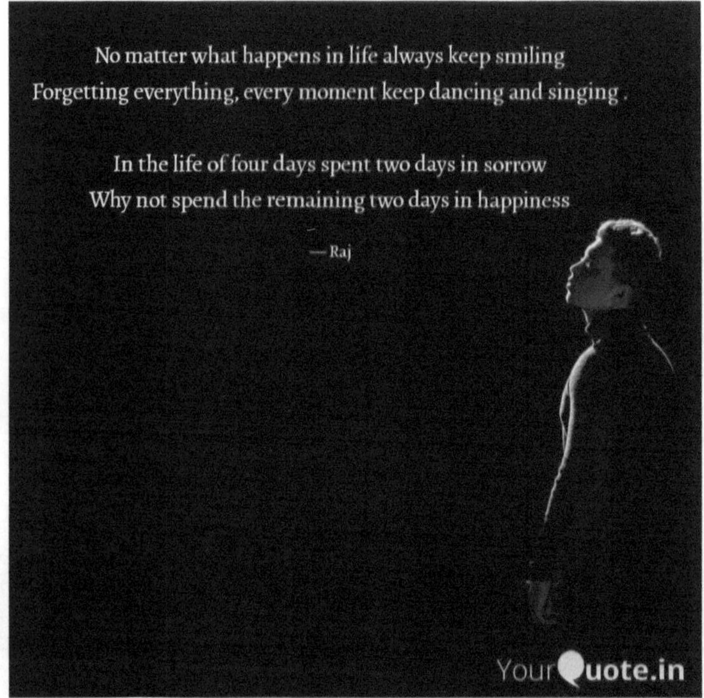

No matter what happens in life always keep smiling
Forgetting everything, every moment keep dancing and singing .

In the life of four days spent two days in sorrow
Why not spend the remaining two days in happiness

—Raj

Your Quote.in

65. No pain is bigger than

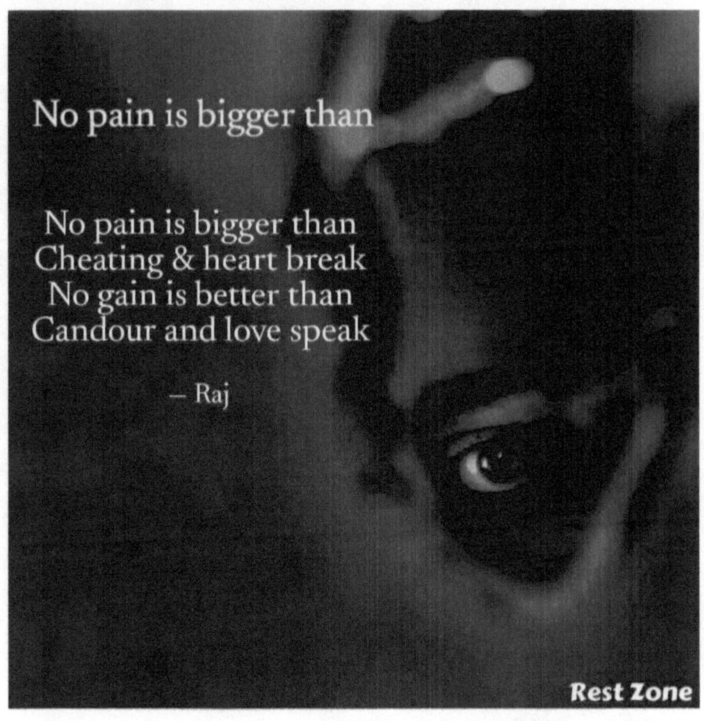

No pain is bigger than

No pain is bigger than
Cheating & heart break
No gain is better than
Candour and love speak

— Raj

Rest Zone

66. Nothing stays the same

Nothing stays the same after

Nothing stays the same after
Having a mid night shower
Freshness booms as never
Vanishing tiredness forever

Nothing stays the same after
The dark that end's forever
Filling the brightness all over
Creating happiness as never

Nothing stays the same after
The hardship and the fervor
Hoping for a change to occur
In the changing world forever

— Raj

67. Separation

हिज्र / Separation

The pain of separation
Can't be said in a sentence

Dwelling of pain in the heart
Keeps hurting time to time

— Raj

Rest Zone

68. People change like

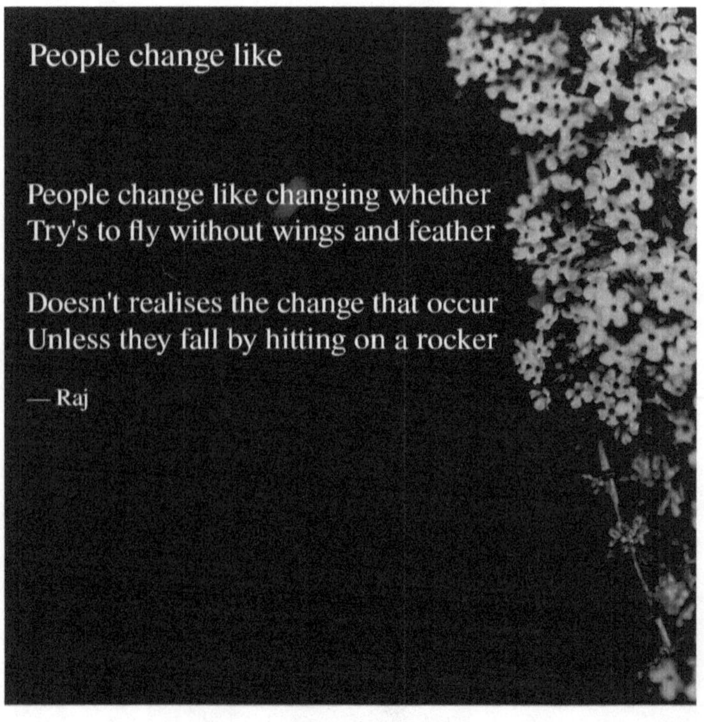

People change like

People change like changing whether
Try's to fly without wings and feather

Doesn't realises the change that occur
Unless they fall by hitting on a rocker

— Raj

69. Life is full of lessons

Life is full of lessons
People full of treasons

Every day is a chapter
Learn it in full vigour

It teaches new colour
Every day every hour

— Raj

70. Positive thoughts help

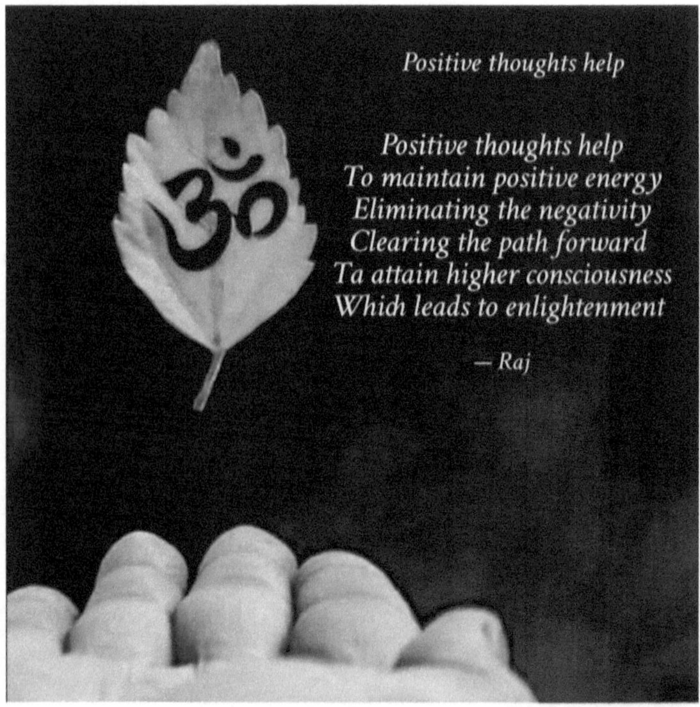

Positive thoughts help

Positive thoughts help
To maintain positive energy
Eliminating the negativity
Clearing the path forward
Ta attain higher consciousness
Which leads to enlightenment

— Raj

71. What is beauty?

What is beauty?
The quality of a person
Which gives pleasure
To the mind, soul and senses
Is called beauty

Physical appearances doesn't
Constitutes to beauty

- Raj

72. Morning dews

Watching the morning dew
Garden where flower blooms

You are my beloved flower
Never gloom always bloom

Roses, Lilies, Jasmine, mogra
Air filled with mixed aroma

I can hear the birds singing
Viewing the different colours

I can see the bees roaming
Around the flower for nectar

Nature has got it's own glory
Showering different colours
–Raj

73. Some love stories

Some love stories

Some love stories
Will never end
Some love stories
Has a tragic end
While some are never told
And buried in hearts coffin
While some doesn't see
The sunlight

— Raj

74. Star-eyed Mayna

Star-eyed wild myna
There is no pleassure without you
In this midnight of loneliness
What a pleasure to hear voice of you

— Raj

75. What is Solitude?

What is solitude?

The state of being alone
Feeling pleasant and at home

Where there is no crowd
without being someone around

Staying all day introverted
Liking the peace that surround

— Raj

76. Tears rolling down

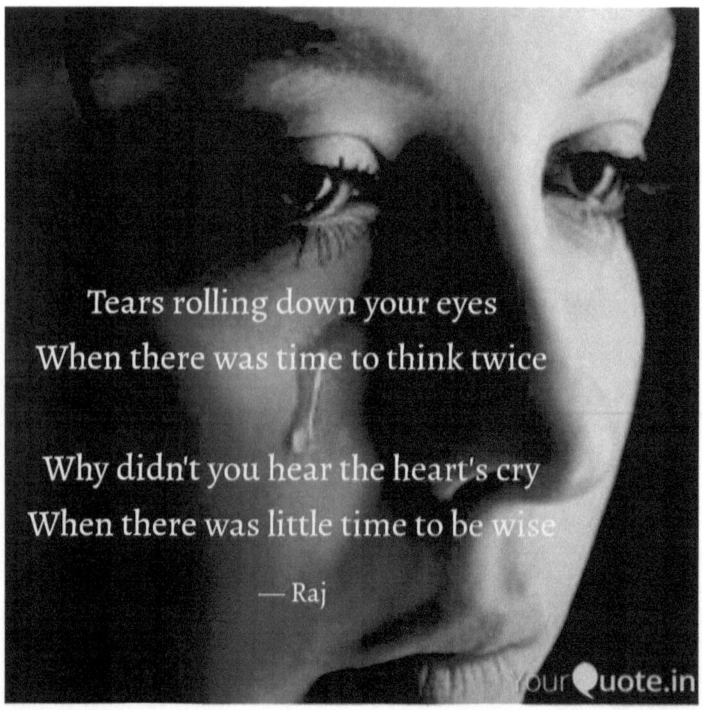

Tears rolling down your eyes
When there was time to think twice

Why didn't you hear the heart's cry
When there was little time to be wise

— Raj

77. Whenever something ends

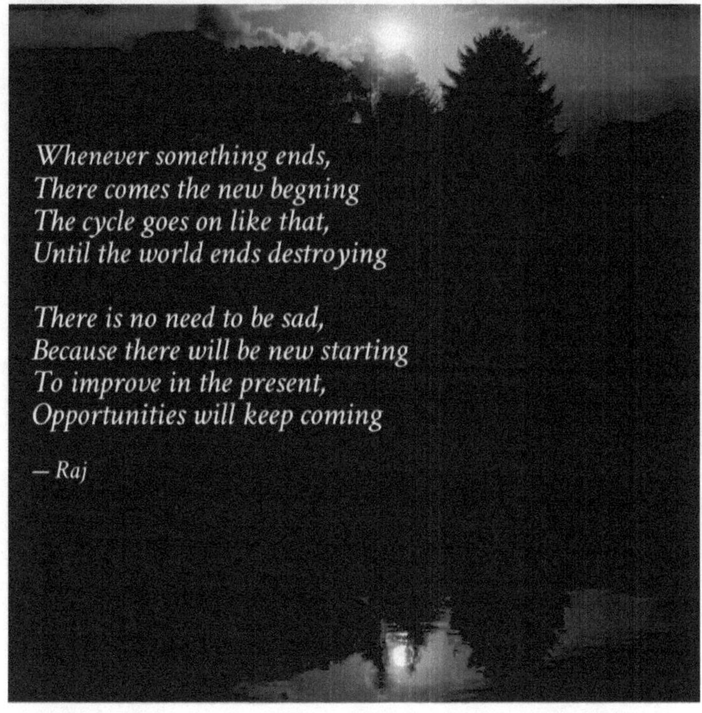

Whenever something ends,
There comes the new begning
The cycle goes on like that,
Until the world ends destroying

There is no need to be sad,
Because there will be new starting
To improve in the present,
Opportunities will keep coming

— Raj

78. There are emotions

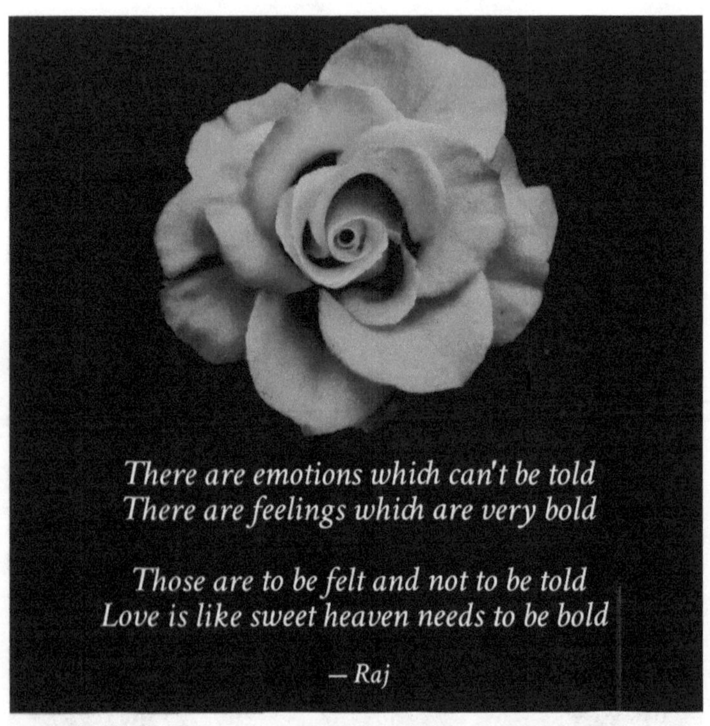

There are emotions which can't be told
There are feelings which are very bold

Those are to be felt and not to be told
Love is like sweet heaven needs to be bold

— Raj

79. If there were no oceans

If there were no oceans,
People would have died due to dehydrations
There would have been no life existence
No rains and no plants except aliens
Earth would have been like another planet
Where there is no life and only land

— Raj

YourQuote.in

80. The power of destiny

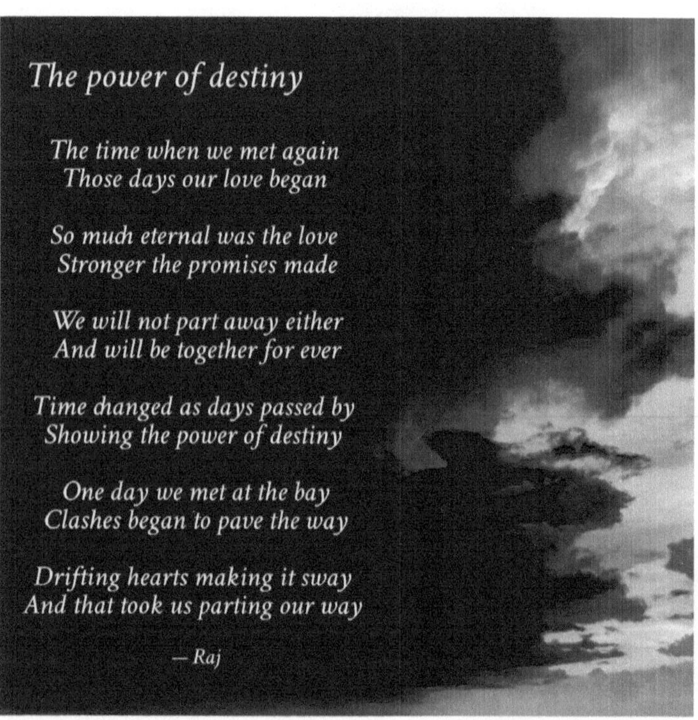

The power of destiny

The time when we met again
Those days our love began

So much eternal was the love
Stronger the promises made

We will not part away either
And will be together for ever

Time changed as days passed by
Showing the power of destiny

One day we met at the bay
Clashes began to pave the way

Drifting hearts making it sway
And that took us parting our way

— Raj

81. Life is a railway track

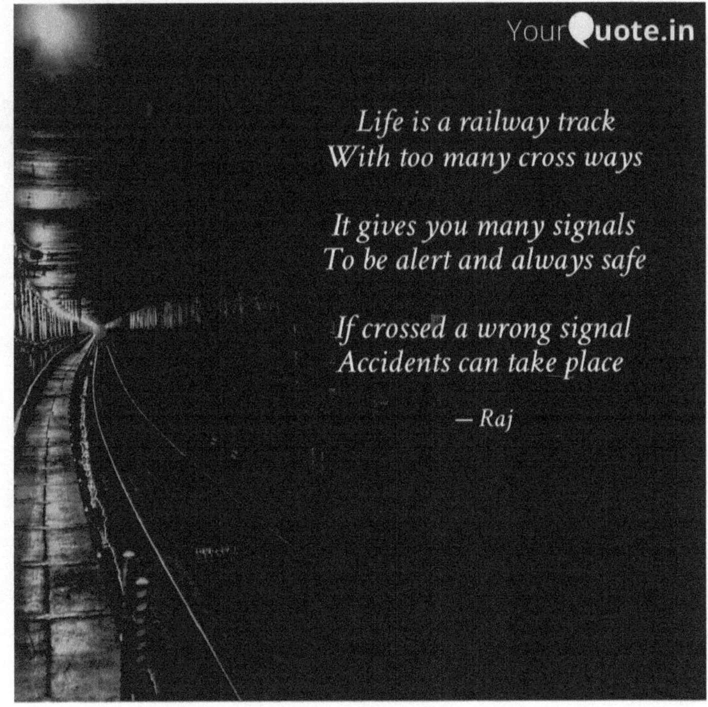

Life is a railway track
With too many cross ways

It gives you many signals
To be alert and always safe

If crossed a wrong signal
Accidents can take place

— Raj

82. True friendship

True friendship

True friendship always blooms
Like a flower it never glooms

It's like a whole lifetime process
Once it begins it never end's

— Raj

83. Try-try but don't cry

#Try#

The world says try-try but don't cry
But does they know how much I try
The world says patience is a must
But does they know how much I trust
The world says new begning will open
But does they know when will it happen
The world says changes are going to come
But does they say what changes are welcome
It is easier to say something
But difficult to implement

— Raj

YourQuote.in

84. To understand my silence

To understand my silence,

To understand my silence
One should have intelligence

Seeing my every elegance
Know body language in a glance

Should understand the essence
Before making out the sentence

— Raj

85. What's unique about her

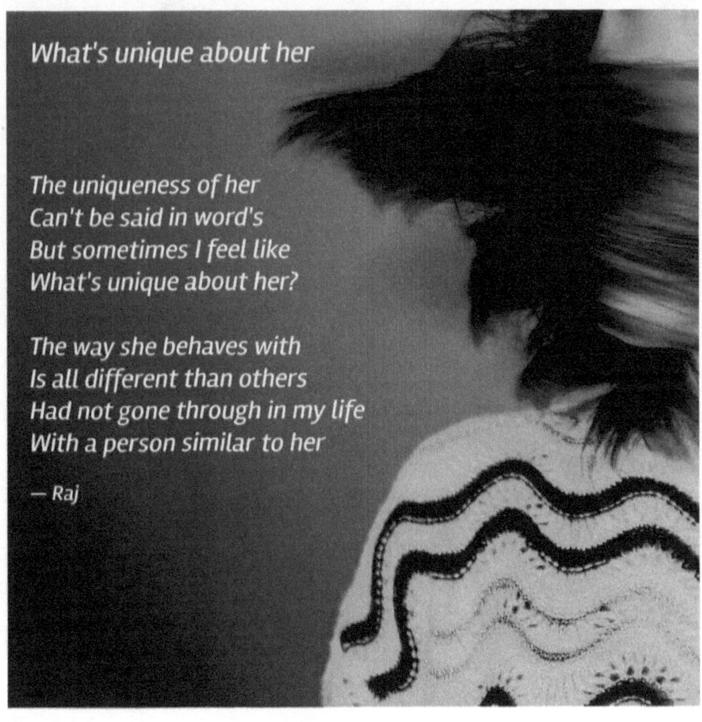

What's unique about her

The uniqueness of her
Can't be said in word's
But sometimes I feel like
What's unique about her?

The way she behaves with
Is all different than others
Had not gone through in my life
With a person similar to her

— Raj

86. A voice echoes

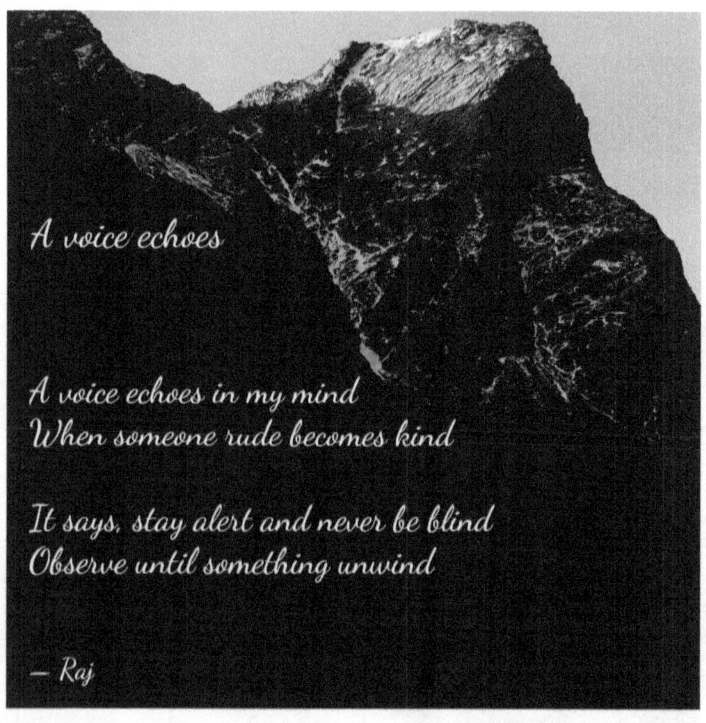

A voice echoes

A voice echoes in my mind
When someone rude becomes kind

It says, stay alert and never be blind
Observe until something unwind

— Raj

87. Walking alone

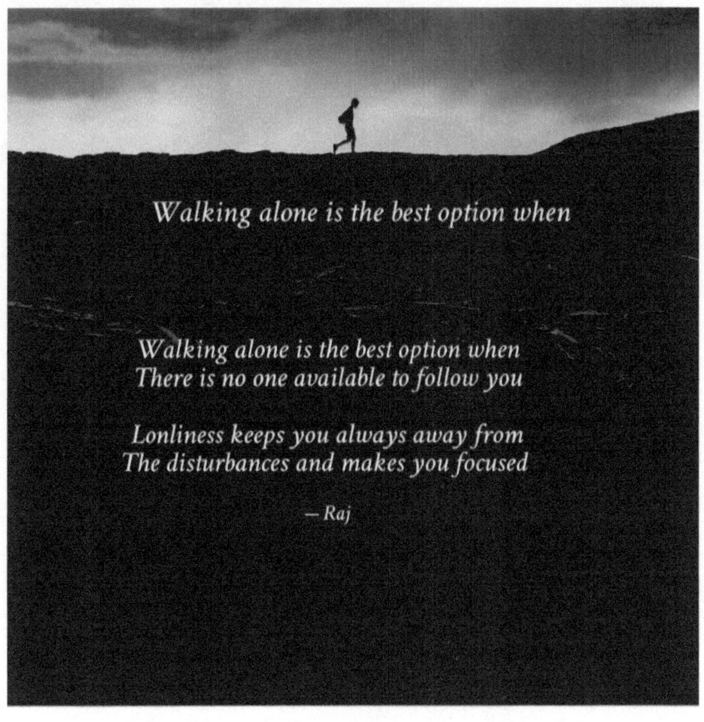

Walking alone is the best option when

Walking alone is the best option when
There is no one available to follow you

Lonliness keeps you always away from
The disturbances and makes you focused

— Raj

88. War and peace are like

War and peace are like

War and peace are like
Two sides of the same coin
War brings destructions
While peace brings restrictions

War means loss of lives
While peace means gain on lives
War brings loss of inventory
While peace makes lot of inventory

— Raj

89. I fell in love with

I fell in love with
The way the life plays
Giving intermittent challanges
By bringing you on cross roads

because
It makes a person strong enough
To live playing the game
Which is called life
without taking it serious

—Raj

YourQuote.in

90. Some things never change

Some things never change
Whatever the circumstances maybe
However a person tries to be
Everything remains the same
Unchanged and unaffected

— Raj

91. Whenever I think of you

Whenever I think of you,

When ever I think of you
My heart beats faster
Memories get overloaded
By the moments we shared

— Raj

92. When I am with her

YourQuote.in

When I am with her I feel like

When I am with her I feel like
I am cold and warmness strike
Being in heaven is a small thing
Which makes me crave everything

— Raj

93. The pain of separation

The pain of separation

When there is no one
Think that you are someone

Born alone in this world
Has to go alone from this world

The pain of seperation happens
When you get attached to someone

Between the period of Life and death
People come and go very often

Remember that no one stays attached
We are travelers and they are passerby's

— Raj

94. When we trust someone

Rest Zone

When we trust someone

When we trust someone
We believe them fully
When there is a trust breach
Our heart breaks fully

— Raj

95. When you said

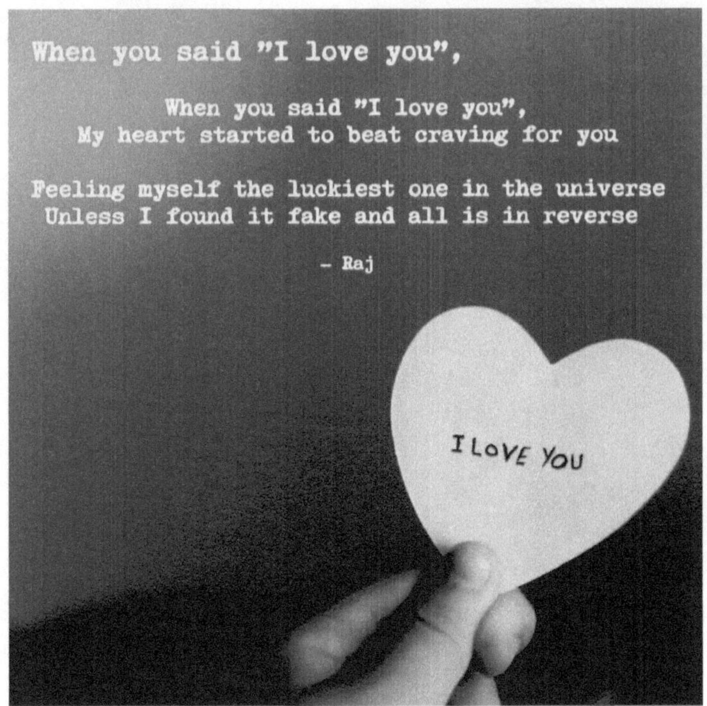

When you said "I love you",

When you said "I love you",
My heart started to beat craving for you

Feeling myself the luckiest one in the universe
Unless I found it fake and all is in reverse

- Raj

I LOVE YOU

96. When you walk alone

When you walk alone,

When you walk alone,
Don't be rigid as a stone

Life is a bit hard to digest
Will go on smooth I suggest

Let go along with the flow
Don't haste and be slow

When there is a day after night
After darkness comes the bright

— Raj

97. Where there is suffering

Where there is suffering,

Where there is suffering,
There won't be any gathering
People vacate on the spot
Leaving you behind laughing

The world has changed a lot
Leaving you in solitude to rot
Without anyone to help you
Making you grieve and clot

— Raj

98. If you had loved me

• 98 •

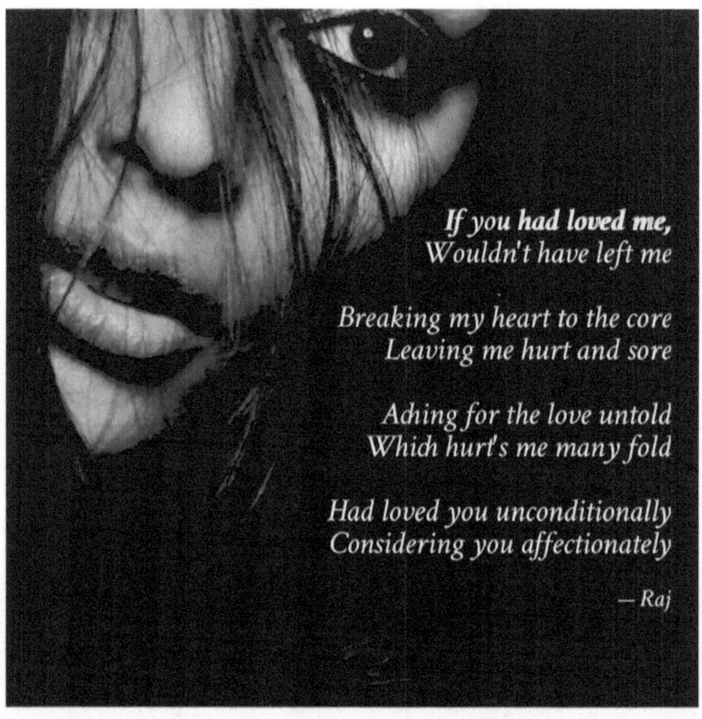

If you **had loved me,**
Wouldn't have left me

Breaking my heart to the core
Leaving me hurt and sore

Aching for the love untold
Which hurt's me many fold

Had loved you unconditionally
Considering you affectionately

— Raj

99. You are the reason why I smile

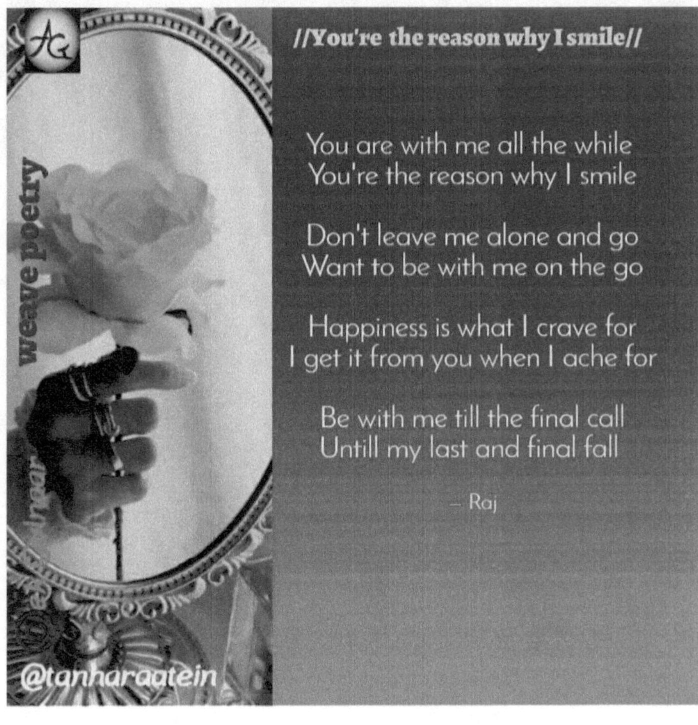

//You're the reason why I smile//

You are with me all the while
You're the reason why I smile

Don't leave me alone and go
Want to be with me on the go

Happiness is what I crave for
I get it from you when I ache for

Be with me till the final call
Untill my last and final fall

– Raj

Weave poetry

@tanharaatein

100. Your past is like

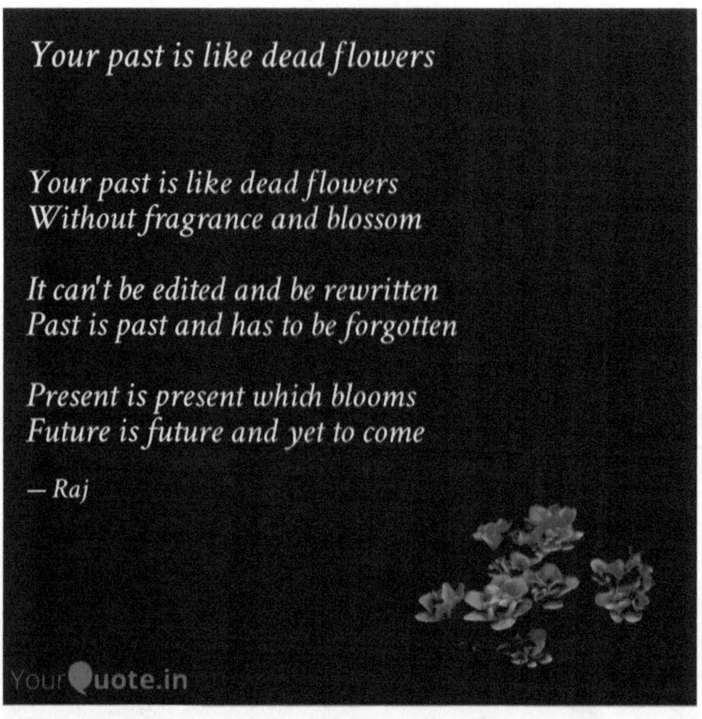

Your past is like dead flowers

Your past is like dead flowers
Without fragrance and blossom

It can't be edited and be rewritten
Past is past and has to be forgotten

Present is present which blooms
Future is future and yet to come

— Raj

Disclaimer

All creations are based on fiction. It has nothing to do with the life of the author or anyone in the universe. All articles are fictitious and bear no resemblance to any person living or dead. If there is any similarity, it is just coincidence.

Author's Bio

Mr. K. C. Shreeraj Menon born to an affluent family in Kerala on 09th September 1973 to Mr. Kozhipurath Sankunni Menon and Mrs. Kizhara Chalapurath Sethulakshmi Menon and Domiciled in Maharashtra. From childhood, he used to make quick poetry, say and forget it. A close friend of his once noticed this and forced him to write whatever Poems or Quotes he used to say and since then he started writing. He kept his poetry and Quotes to himself and his close friends until he found a platform to write his works online. He is an active writer on Your Quote site and has received numerous testimonials and certifications for the contest. He is a multilingual writer and his writing is awe-inspiring. Be it English, Hindi, Urdu, Malayalam and Marathi, he excels in all languages. He is also a great inspiration to many intriguing writers. He is a graduate from Mumbai University. He is an accountant and also a self-educated computer engineer. His skills are top notch and he holds several certifications. His passions are acting, writing, painting and dance and listening to music etc… etc….

Mail Id:- shreeraj_m@yahoo.co.uk